DEATH Penalty
A Curse To Society ?

Author- Yash Rawat
Instagram: *yash_writer05*

Title Verso

Title: Death Penalty: A Curse To Society?

Author: Yash Rawat

Copyright © 2024 by Yash Rawat

All rights reserved, including the right of reproduction, in whole, or in part in any form. To be published as an ebook and as a paperback.

Publisher: Yash Rawat

ISBN: 9798342626064

Price: $ 9.99

Disclaimer

This book's content stems from thorough research and examination of data available through July 2024. Keep in mind that the information and viewpoints shared here aim to inform and spark thought, not to upset or damage any community, group, or nation. The opinions expressed belong to the author and come from unbiased research and data.

The book doesn't try to keep stereotypes going or push any kind of discrimination. We ask readers to look at the material with an open mind and think about the context it was written in. The author recognizes the range of viewpoints and the intricacy of the topics discussed. Any offense taken isn't on purpose, and the author stays committed to encouraging respectful conversation and understanding.

CONTENTS

1. Introduction — 01
2. History — 07
3. Methods — 17
4. Scenario in India — 30
5. A curse? — 50

INTRODUCTION

Death

One of the most feared things in the world is Death. It is an absolute truth and none can escape it. This fear is used to curb crimes committed by humans from time immemorial. As time passed and we developed more civic sense, the methods of execution became less cruel, and the number of crimes punishable by death also reduced.

Death penalty

The death penalty is imposed on a person or a group of persons after they are found guilty of a crime whose nature is so heinous that other punishment such as life imprisonment would seem unjustifiable. Some crimes are very cruel in nature, like terrorism, multiple murders, murder by torture etc. In these crimes, life imprisonment would not fully suffice as the punishment and death penalty is imposed as a justifiable alternative.

This also gives some relief and satisfaction to the family and friends of the victims. This fosters a sense of societal retribution and sets an example intended to stop individuals from committing such heinous crimes in the future.

Present Scenario

At present, the number of persons executed by India are significantly lower compared to those in the U.S.A and China.

The last execution in India was in 2020, the execution of four rapists of the Nirbhaya case. As I am writing this the last time the U.S.A. executed a person was in January 2024, whereas China executed the most recent person in July 2024.

Till now India has executed only 8 persons in the 21st century which is very low when compared to more than one hundred in U.S.A. and China. This indicates that India is less inclined to hang people as compared to other nations.

Currently there are 114 countries which have completely abolished the death penalty. While there are many nations that have not performed any executions in the past decade but still have the provision for executing people in their laws. Also, there are many countries that have abolished the death penalty for most of the crimes. There are a few unofficial reports that some countries still execute people in public.

The possibility of a death sentence can come across as a justifiable punishment for several offenses, though some are executed for completely unjustifiable reasons such as drug peddling, blasphemy or homosexuality.

According to a report from Amnesty International a total of 1153 executions were recorded around the globe in the year 2023 while in the year 2022 there were 883 executions. The executions in the year 2021 and 2020 were 579 and 483 respectively. This shows an increasing trend of executions around the globe.

The country that leads in executing people in the world is China and the true numbers cannot be known as the exact official data is not available. According to some unofficial sources, which I cannot confirm, the execution rate is more than 1000 people per annum. The country that leads after China is Iran, which executed 853 people in the year 2023. The third position is taken by Saudi Arabia, which performed 172 executions in the year 2023. It is followed by Somalia and U.S.A. which executed 38 and 24 people respectively in the year 2023. The number of women executed compared to men is also very low around the globe.

Looking at the statistics it's essential to have a clear understanding of capital punishments, its ways of execution, abuses and kinds of crimes that can lead one to the death penalty.

Organizations

Nowadays, many international and human rights groups are fighting for the abolishment of the death penalty around the globe. These include: Amnesty International, the World Coalition Against the Death Penalty, the International Commission Against the Death Penalty, and many more.

These organizations promote worldwide governments in their measure to do away with the death penalty in laws and at the same time providing useful statistics that are collected through research.

HISTORY

Brief introduction

As we look back through history, we observe that methods of execution were often increasingly cruel and pervasive. In some cases, individuals could receive the death penalty even for minor offenses.

Those were the days when monarchy was prevalent and no one could question the authority of the king. In order to rule with an iron foot, occasionally public executions were conducted in order to create an environment of fear among ordinary people, which, though, sowed the seeds of hatred for the king in their hearts, but at the same time, fear also grew with it.

The methods of execution were notably inhumane and designed to spread maximum fear. The exploitation of the poor was widespread, but the pervasive fear of death effectively stifled any potential rebellion.

Religion also played a significant role in shaping laws related to execution. Many religious texts outlined their own laws, which were followed by rulers. For instance, Islamic law (Sharia) prescribed specific punishments, while Buddhists were strictly against the death penalty and so it was not in practice in the empires ruled by the Buddhist kings.

A Look at History

For clarity, history can be divided into two main sections:

1. Ancient History

2. **Modern History**

Ancient History

The earliest use of the death penalty can be traced back to ancient times, possibly as far back as the Satya Yuga. Although detailed codified laws are scarce, it is known that kings often imposed death sentences based on their judgment, though infrequently. In the Dwapara Yuga and Treta Yuga, similar procedures were followed. In early Kali Yuga, the death penalty was applied for crimes such as murder, treason, and adultery. During the Mauryan era, due to Buddhist influence the death penalty was abolished, and the Gupta Empire followed the same.

The first codified laws concerning the death penalty are provided in the Code of King Hammurabi of Babylon, which dates back to the 18th century BCE. It prescribed *the death penalty for 25 different kinds of crimes, though murder was not included therein.*

The Code of Nesilim, composed between 1650-1500 BCE, allowed capital punishment for a variety of crimes, including sex crimes.

Ancient Egyptian law allowed for the death penalty in cases of murder, adultery in certain situations, and treason.

Ancient Chinese methods of execution were particularly brutal, with prisoners of war facing extreme forms of punishment. Some other crimes punishable by death were offenses committed against family members, like killing or selling relatives into slavery.

The Draconian Code, written almost around the 8th century BCE in Athens, ordered the death punishment for all crimes making it one of the most extreme laws ever recorded in history.

The ancient Roman Empire is notorious for its unique and cruel methods of execution, crucifixion being one of them. Generally murderers and betrayers were executed.

Modern History

After having introduced the antiquities let us now proceed to modern times with special reference to India.

Mughal and Maratha Period

The law system utilized during the Islamic reign in India was based on Sharia law, which provides punishments according to Islamic standards.

In lieu of that, various crimes including homicide and treason attract capital punishment under Hindu empires like the Maratha Empire. On the other hand, public shaming was done in place of the death penalty onto women. Similarly Brahmins were not hanged but instead imprisoned under rough conditions until they died while their land was taken away from them.

Some prominent executions during this time include:

- **Guru Tegh Bahadur:** Beheaded in Chandni Chowk, he was the ninth Sikh Guru. His associates Bhai Mati Das (sawn into two), Bhai Dayal Das (boiled alive) and Bhai Sati Das (dismembered) were also killed.
- **Guru Arjan Dev:** The fifth Sikh Guru, executed by Mughal Emperor Jahangir.
- **Shambhuraje:** The second Maratha king, tortured and executed by Mughal Emperor Aurangzeb. His body was allegedly dismembered and thrown into a river. His companion, Kavi Kalash Dev, was also executed in the same way.

British Era

Execution by hanging became an increasingly prevalent form of punishment during the British colonial rule in India. In order to quell uprisings, however, rebels were frequently dealt with by shooting or by being blown from a cannon; such execution involves fastening a person at the mouth of a cannon which is then fired. Many of those executed by the British were freedom fighters.

Notable figures include:

- ***Maharaja Nandakumar:*** *Executed on August 5, 1775, for forgery. He was the first person to be executed by the Britishers. He was a tax collector in the region of Bengal. His execution is often referred to as 'judicial murder.' It is important to* note that he was not a king; the title 'Maharaja' was conferred by Shah Alam II.

- **Bhagat Singh, Shivaram Rajguru, and Sukhdev Thapar:** Prominent figures in the Indian freedom struggle, hanged by the British Indian government on March 23, 1931.
- **Khudiram Bose:** An Indian nationalist from Bengal, executed on August 11, 1908. He was the youngest person to be executed in India.
- **Mangal Pandey:** He was a sepoy in the 34th Bengal native infantry who started the Indian rebellion of 1857. He was executed on 8th April 1857 by hanging.
- **Tatya Tope:** Tatya Tope was a trusted commander of Rani Lakshmibai of Jhansi. He played a major role in the Indian rebellion of 1857 and was subsequently hanged on 18th April 1859.

There were very few executions of British individuals. British casualties were minimal. A notable case is that of **George Flaxman** of the Leicestershire Regiment, who was executed for the murder of Lance Sergeant William Carmody in Lucknow on January 10, 1887. The action inspired Rudyard Kipling's famous poem 'Danny Deever'.

Conclusion

This history of capital punishment and how it's changed shows a past full of major abuse and brutality. In the past, executions scared people more than they delivered justice. Today's democracies use the death penalty less often and with more rules. Now, it's to serve justice, not to frighten people. Courts still give death sentences, but they are often commuted to life in prison.

This shows a move towards kinder treatment and an understanding of past wrongs. Many times, people lost *their lives for small crimes sometimes without proper trials. These were still common in the British era and many freedom fighters were executed without any proper or fair trial.*

Methods

Introduction

As noted in the second chapter, as we look further back in time the execution methods have become more brutal and frequent. In this chapter, we will explore the execution methods in ancient and modern times.

I will divide this chapter into two sections for your convenience:

i) **Methods used in the past**

ii) **Methods used in the present**

Methods used in past times

The main methods used for execution in the past were:

1. ***Guillotine****: This device was used to carry out executions by beheading. It consists of a tall frame with a weighted and angled blade attached to the top. The person to be executed was secured in a pillory (a device with three holes to secure the hands and head in place, preventing any movement) at the bottom of the frame. The blade was then released, swiftly decapitating the person.*

   The device was made to guarantee a death without pain, because the head was chopped off with one blow. It was considered to be less cruel than the earlier punishment called the breaking wheel.

   This method was employed in executing King Louis XVI and Queen Marie Antoinette in the year 1793.

Employed broadly during the French Revolution, it was France's official method of execution until 1981 when capital punishment was abolished.

2. **Breaking Wheel**: Also known as the execution wheel, this was a large and heavy wooden wheel used for wooden carts and carriages. The convict was first tied to the floor to prevent resistance or movement, then the wheel was used to break the bones of the body. Eventually the wheel was either dropped on the neck or chest to end their life, or the person was left tied to the wheel and erected to die a painful death.

This method is one of the oldest and most gruesome forms of execution in Europe, intended not just to end life but to torture the convict.

The execution of Bhai Subheg Singh and Bhai Shahbaz Singh was conducted on a rotating wheel *in 1746. The last known execution by this method or its variant occurred in Prussia in 1841.*

3. **Crucifixion**: *This method involves nailing the convict to a large wooden cross and leaving them to die. Death is accompanied by agonizing pain and suffering, which can potentially take several days. Causes of death could include dehydration, infection from the wounds (caused by nails), exhaustion, or hypovolemic shock. Birds and rats might feast on the open wounds, leading to further complications.*

This method was used in Europe, Persia, Japan, Burma, and surrounding areas. According to Christian mythology, Jesus Christ was executed by this method under Roman rule. Under Sharia law, crucifixion is still a rare method of execution in Saudi Arabia, and Sudan's penal code also includes it as a penalty.

4. **Impalement**: In the process of carrying out this form of torture-death, a long pointed wooden stick or spear is driven into somebody's body from the anus and then pulled out through their mouth. It is one of the most terrifying and horrendous means of killing that human beings have invented over time, and sometimes people who are being punished may remain alive for several days before death arrives. This method was widely used in ancient Egypt and various parts of ancient Europe.

5. **Electric Chair and Lethal Gas**: The electric chair and gas chamber were historically used for executions in the U.S.A., with lethal gas also employed by Nazi Germany, the Soviet Union, and Lithuania.

Although these methods are not widely used today, they remain legal options in some U.S. states. The electric chair, invented by Alfred P. Southwick, a New York dentist, involves strapping the condemned to a wooden chair and electrocuting them via electrodes attached to the head and legs. This method is known for being extremely painful, often requiring multiple shocks.

The gas chamber executes the condemned with lethal gas, such as hydrogen cyanide or carbon monoxide, in an airtight chamber. This method often led to severe pain and took several minutes to cause death.

Both methods have largely been replaced by lethal injection in the U.S., but they remain legal options in some states.

6. **Mazzatello**: This method of execution that is brutal and vicious is referred to as mazzatello and it includes tying the condemned person to a chair so

as to pound his head with a heavy hammer. Most of the time the condemned would not die immediately but just faint so they slit their neck with a knife.

7. **Blowing from a Gun**: The convict was tied to the mouth of a cannon, which was then fired. This method was used during the colonial era, particularly by the British and the Portuguese in their colonies.

8. **Burning and Boiling**: In burning, the condemned was tied to a pole or stake and burned alive. This method was used in ancient Europe and America.

The boiling method involved immersing the condemned in boiling liquid, such as water, oil, or tar. This method was practiced in parts of Europe and Asia.

9. **Keelhauling**: Used mainly by pirates and sailors, the convict was dragged through the water under the keel of a ship, dying either from drowning or from injuries sustained from the keel.

10. **By Swords**: The convict was beheaded or mutilated according to the severity of the crime. This was a common method of execution worldwide.

Methods used in present times

The main methods used for execution in the present time are:

1. **Hanging**: It is the most common method of execution globally. It has two known methods: short drop and long drop.

The short drop method involves making the convict stand on a support with a noose around their neck, then removing the support, leading to death by suffocation. This method is painful and slow compared to the long drop method.

The long drop method, invented by William Marwood in 1892 in Britain, aims to break the convict's neck to cause immediate unconsciousness and rapid brain death. The height of the fall is calculated based on the convict's weight to ensure that the energy produced is enough to break the neck without causing decapitation. This method is considered less painful and is currently used in India.

2. **Lethal Injection**: This approach is relatively recent and practiced in nations such as U.S.A, Taiwan, Vietnam, Nigeria, Maldives and China.

Julius Mount Bleyer, a doctor from New York proposed this in 1888 where three drugs are injected in sequence. So first one is sodium thiopental (an anesthetic that makes one unconscious), the next is pancuronium bromide (a muscle relaxant that leads to paralysis and finally asphyxiation), and lastly potassium chloride (which causes heart failure). The person who is going to be executed takes approximately seven minutes to die.

This technique is deemed less agonizing generally although some complaints have been raised about how painful it can be if the anesthetic fails to perform well enough as the potassium chloride can cause severe pain.

3. **Firing Squad**: *In this method, a group of shooters aims at the heart of the convict . Typically, only one*

rifle is loaded with a bullet to maintain anonymity among the shooters.

The convict may be made unconscious with anesthetics (though not all countries use anesthetics), then strapped to a chair, and the shooters fire. If anesthetics are not used, this method can be painful and sometimes results in prolonged death if the shooters miss the heart.

4. **Beheading**: Prevalent in Saudi Arabia, this method involves decapitation with a sharp sword.
5. **Stoning**: In this method, a group of people throws rocks or stones at the convict until death. The countries which still have such punishment in their laws include Afghanistan, Burundi, Iran , Iraq, Nigeria , Saudi Arabia , Pakistan , Sudan , Yemen and Somalia. Today it is one of the cruelest and most barbaric means of execution.

6. **Nitrogen Hypoxia**: This is one of the latest and most painless methods of execution. The convicts wear a respirator mask in which breathing air is replaced with pure nitrogen, leading to unconsciousness within minutes and eventually death from lack of oxygen. As I am writing this, it is used only once in the execution of Kenneth Smith in January 2024 in U.S.A.

Conclusion

It can be concluded that methods of execution were extremely cruel in ancient times. Even in the 20th century, methods such as the electric chair were particularly nightmarish. Over time, execution methods have become less harsh. For example, in France, the breaking wheel was replaced by the guillotine, which was comparatively less cruel. Similarly, the short drop method was replaced by the long drop method, and methods like the electric chair and lethal gas have been succeeded by letnal injection and nitrogen hypoxia.

Today, most methods of execution aim to minimize pain, with the notable exception cf stoning. This shift reflects a move away from using executions as a means to instill fear and towards focusing solely on punishment.

Scenario in India

Introduction

The death penalty in India has been practiced for centuries, with its history detailed in the second chapter.

In 2015, the National Law University Delhi compiled a list of individuals executed in India since independence and concluded that at least 752 individuals have been executed. However, this data is not entirely reliable as many state authorities have reported losing old records.

Raghuraj Singh alias Rasha was the first person to be executed in independent India on 9th September 1947 at Jabalpur Central Jail. The latest ones were Akshay Thakur, Mukesh Singh, Pawan Gupta and Vinay Sharma executed on March 20, 2020 at Tihar Jail. Rattan Bai Jain, executed on 3 January 1955 at Tihar Jail, is presumed to be the first woman executed in independent India.

Currently, the death penalty in India is prescribed for various offenses under the Bharatiya Nyay Sanhita.

These offenses include:

Section under BNS	Nature of crime
§ 65(2) of BNS	Rape of a child below 12 years of age
§ 66 of BNS	Rape and injury which causes death or leaves a woman in a Persistent Vegetative State

§ 70(2) of BNS	Gang rape of a child under 18 years of age
§ 71 of BNS	Repeat offenses in the context of rape
§ 103(1) of BNS	Murder
§ 103(2) of BNS	Lynching
§ 104 of BNS	Murder by prisoner serving life sentence
§ 107 of BNS	Abetment of suicide of a child or a person of unsound mind
§ 109(2) of BNS	Attempted murder by prisoner serving life sentence
§ 111(2)(a) of BNS	Organized crime offenses causing death

§ 113(2)(a) of BNS	Terrorism resulting in the death of any person
§ 140(2) of BNS	Kidnapping or abducting in order to murder or for ransom
§ 147 of BNS	Treason against the Government of India
§ 160 of BNS	Abetment of mutiny, if mutiny is actually committed in consequence
§ 230(2) of BNS	Giving or fabricating false evidence with intent to procure conviction of capital offence resulting in death of innocent person
§ 232(2) of BNS	Threatening any person to give false evidence resulting in death of innocent person

§ 310(3) of BNS	Felony murder while committing dacoity or banditry

Other acts that have the provision of death penalty include:

Act	Section	Nature of crime
Army Act, 1950	34	Offences in relation to enemy and punishable with death
Army Act, 1950	37	Mutiny
Army Act, 1950	38 (1)	Desertion
Assam Rifles Act, 2006	21	Offences in relation to enemy and punishable with death

Assam Rifles Act, 2006	24	Mutiny
Assam Rifles Act, 2006	25 (1) (a)	Desertion
Assam Rifles Act, 2006	55	Civil offences
Bombay Prohibition (Gujarat Amendment) Act, 2009	65A (2)	Death caused by the consumption of Laththa
Border Security Force Act, 1968	14	Offences in relation to the enemy and punishable with death

Border Security Force Act, 1968	*17*	*Mutiny*
Border Security Force Act, 1968	*18 (1) (a)*	*Desertion*
Border Security Force Act, 1968	*46*	*Civil offences*
Coast Guard Act, 1978	*17*	*Mutiny*
Coast Guard Act, 1978	*49*	*Civil offences*
The Commission of Sati (Prevention) Act, 1987	*41*	*Abetment of sati*

The Defence of India, Act, 1971	5	Person contravening with intent to wage war or assist external aggression or any violation of provision made under Section 3
The Geneva Convention Act 1960	3	Grave breaches of Geneva Conventions
The Explosive Substances Act, 1908	3 (b)	Punishment for special category of offences relating to explosive substances, likely to danger life or cause serious harm
The Indo-Tibetan Border Police Force, Act 1992	16	Offences in relation to enemy or terrorist

The Indo-Tibetan Border Police Force, Act 1992	19	Mutiny
The Indo-Tibetan Border Police Force, Act 1992	20 (1) (a)	Desertion
The Indo-Tibetan Border Police Force, Act 1992	49	Civil offences
The Karnataka Control of Organised Crime Act, 2000	3 (1) (i)	Organized crime resulting in death of person
The Maharashtra Control of	3 (1) (i)	Organized crime resulting in death of person

Organised Crime Act, 1999		
The Narcotics Drugs and Psychotropic Substances Act, 1985	31A (1)	Repeated commission of offences involving commercial quantity of any narcotic drug or psychotropic substance
Maritime Anti-Piracy Act, 2022.	3	Person in committing the act of piracy causes death or an attempt

Handing of death penalty

The death sentence is not always handed down to the offenders of the aforementioned crimes. According to the Indian Constitution there is no express provision for a mandatory death penalty. In fact the death penalty is awarded only in the rarest of rare cases. In Prajeet Kumar Singh vs. State of Bihar, Supreme Court indicated when would be such 'rarest of rare case'. These are murder that are committed so brutally, grotesquely, diabolically, revoltingly or dastardly that arouse intense and extreme indignation from the community.

Even if lower courts hand out a death sentence it does not necessarily mean that the convict would die. Many death sentences are commuted to life imprisonment. Additionally, many convicts receive a presidential pardon, further commutating their sentences to life imprisonment.

The execution of convicts is not a straightforward process and sometimes requires significant societal involvement, as evidenced by the recent executions of the four Nirbhaya rapists, which prompted widespread protests across the country.

Procedure of handing death penalty

Firstly, the trial court sets the pace for any death penalty proceedings. A death sentence may be awarded if the convicts are found guilty and if the judge considers it to be a "rarest of rare" case. The court should record the reasons for awarding the death sentence thereby explaining why life imprisonment would be insufficient.

After awarding a death sentence, it is mandatory for the High Court to confirm the same. The decision of the High Court could either confirm or overturn the sentence of death; it may replace it with another penalty; it may modify the charges; it may direct re-trial either on fresh or old charges or may even set free the convict from prison. High Courts also have authority to take over cases which are still pending in lower courts and conduct their trials including awarding capital punishment.

After the High Court confirms the death penalty, it is possible for the convicted person to file an appeal using Special Leave Petition (SLP) in the Supreme Court of India. It is the responsibility of the Supreme Court to determine whether the SLP is worth being considered like an appeal. Notably, special leave petitions involving death sentences cannot be dismissed without providing reasons.

A petition for review of the judgment of the Supreme Court can be filed within a period of 30 days after the judgment over the special leave petition. This petition is heard in open court by a three judge Bench which holds oral hearings limited to 30 minutes.

If the judgment is annulled or disposed of, a curative petition may be made to the Supreme Court in order to have it look at its verdict again on account of violations in principles of natural justice or suspicion about impartiality on part of the judge. If available then, Curative petitions are handled by that same bench who decided the review petition or three senior most justices at the highest court. These petitions are typically disposed of without oral arguments unless the Court directs otherwise.

If all legal remedies are exhausted, the last resort for a convict is to apply for clemency from either the Governor or President of India. A mercy petition must be submitted within thirty days after one has been informed about its rejection of a special leave petition. First it should go to the Governor and if turned down then this should be submitted within 60 days to the President. After receiving such an appeal, recommendations have to be made by the central government within two months. The President's decision must reach both the state and the Superintendent of the concerned Jail within 48 hours.

When every single legal recourse has been pursued and rejected, a death warrant or black warrant is provided by the court. It must be delivered to the Superintendent of the Jail who must send it back with a signed document ensuring that execution has been done. A death warrant states when and where an execution will happen. Usually, these are only given after all legal processes have been used up.

This system consists of very complicated procedures that take too long for execution of any person and prevents the execution of any innocent person. Consequently, it is very rare for a death sentence to be carried out in India.

Condition of the convicts awarded death penalty

As soon as the death sentence is confirmed by the Sessions Court, the convict is treated as an outcast in prison. By law, prisoners sentenced to death are segregated from the general population, though enforcement of this separation varies by state.

Some death row inmates are kept in separate cells reserved for them, searched twice daily, and monitored constantly. The Supreme Court of India has limited solitary confinement to a maximum of 14 days. In many prisons, death row inmates are also restricted from participating in activities or work.

Once the execution is scheduled and a black warrant is issued, death row inmates are placed in isolation, and any objects that could potentially cause self-harm are removed from their cells. Inmates slated for execution *on the same date are prohibited from communicating with each other.*

Fellow inmates often do not live peacefully with death row prisoners, leading to reports of brutality and abuse due to the nature of their crimes. There are also instances where some guards display the gallows and elaborate on the method of execution, further contributing to the inmates' distress.

The delay in court proceedings and the conditions described above contribute to significant psychological torture. Many inmates describe execution as what you will always remember when you stay on death row.

Even after a death row inmate's punishment is converted into life sentence or otherwise acquitted, already what they go through is a heavy price in place of execution. Even those who are close to the prisoners feel horrible as society discards them and they have to bear shame. They often break ties with the convict and do not even accept the body after execution, reflecting the intense stigma attached to being associated with someone condemned to death.

Method of execution

India carries out executions using two methods - hanging and shooting. Shooting is carried out by the Army, Navy, or Air Force only. The decision to use shooting is decided by the court martial.

Before the execution, the executioner performs a dummy test four days prior. The executioner will drop a sandbag (which weighs 1.5 times the weight of the convict) from 1.8 m and then 2.4 m. The rope is tested to ensure it is safe. The length of the rope for a given fall should be the fall plus the measurement of the angle of the rope from the prisoner's jaw to the angle in the beam. Wax or butter is applied to the loop of the rope, and the jail authorities keep two spare hanging ropes ready in case of an accident.

On the day of the execution, the superintendent wakes the convicts at 3:00 a.m. and allows them to freshen up. They are then served breakfast of their choice. After breakfast, a doctor examines them. The convicts are then asked to change into plain cotton attire, their faces are covered with black hoods, and their hands are tied. They are not allowed to see the gallows.

They are escorted to the noose and positioned under the beam. The hangman ties their legs, places the rope around their necks, and draws the bolt. As speaking is prohibited, the superintendent drops a handkerchief as a signal for the executioner to push the lever. The convicts remain in the hanging position for about 30 minutes, after which a doctor checks the bodies to confirm death.

Conclusion

India has neither abolished the death penalty like many nations nor carries out executions as frequently as countries like the U.S.A. and China.

The process in India is long and slow, which further reduces the number of executions. This detailed procedure helps in preventing the execution of innocent individuals, though it results in prolonged suffering for both the guilty and the innocent.

This suggests that the administration of the death penalty in India is able to guard against the risks of wrongful conviction to some degree but the time taken to administer justice should be reduced. As the saying goes, "Justice delayed is justice denied."

A Curse?

Now the question remains: Is the death penalty a curse to society?

We have discussed in detail the history, methods, and process of the death penalty, as well as the nature of crimes that lead to it in India. From this discussion, it can be summarized that if the death penalty is not used merely to instill fear among people but to serve justice by punishing the culprits, it may not be considered a curse.

Nevertheless, no matter how major the judicial system is, errors are unavoidable, and a life is always at stake. The possibility exists that someone erroneously ended up on death row. These wrongful convictions are caused by the use of planted evidence, concealment of evidence and police and prosecutor misconduct. In *such cases, the death penalty can indeed become a curse to society.*

Thus, the concept of the 'necessary evil' aptly captures the essence of the death penalty. It suggests that while the death penalty may have a role in maintaining justice, its potential for irreversible mistakes makes it a contentious and morally challenging aspect of society. Thus, the death penalty persists as a profound and challenging aspect of our justice system, reflecting both the quest for justice and the enduring need for caution.

It can be concluded that the death penalty shows the challenge of balancing justice with human error. It's a necessary evil that reminds us of the care we must take in our pursuit of fairness.

Author's other book:

1. शांतिनगर

www.ingramcontent.com/pod-product-compliance
Lightning Source LLC
Chambersburg PA
CBHW070417230526
45471CB00006B/2859